THE
POWER OF
SIX
SIGMA

An Inspiring Tale of How Six Sigma Is
Transforming the Way We Work

THE
POWER OF
SIX
SIGMA

Subir Chowdhury

DEARBORN™
TRADE

A **Kaplan Professional** Company

This publication is designed to provide accurate and authoritative information in regard to the subject matter covered. It is sold with the understanding that the publisher is not engaged in rendering legal, accounting, or other professional service. If legal advice or other expert assistance is required, the services of a competent professional should be sought.

Senior Acquisitions Editor: Jean Iversen Cook
Senior Managing Editor: Jack Kiburz
Interior Design: Lucy Jenkins
Cover Design: Scott Rattray, Rattray Design
Typesetting: Elizabeth Pitts

Published by Dearborn Trade, a Kaplan Professional Company

Printed in the United States of America

02 03 10 9 8 7

Library of Congress Cataloging-in-Publication Data

Chowdhury, Subir.
  The power of Six Sigma : an inspiring tale of how Six Sigma is transforming the way we work / Subir Chowdhury.
     p.   cm.
  ISBN 0-7931-4434-5 (hard : alk. paper)
  1. Industrial management. I. Title.
HD31 .C514 2001
658—dc21   00-012888

Dearborn Trade books are available at special quantity discounts to use for sales promotions, employee premiums, or educational purposes. Please call our Special Sales Department to order or for more information, at 800-621-9621, ext. 4410, or write to Dearborn Trade Publishing, 155 N. Wacker Drive, Chicago, IL 60606-1719.

ADVANCE PRAISE

"Subir Chowdhury has broken down the often mystical subject of Six Sigma into a very thorough, yet easy read. I believe *The Power of Six Sigma* will do for your customer-centered, profit-driven defect-reduction efforts what *The Goal* did for cycle time reduction and supply chain improvement."

—Steve Gunther, Vice President, Six Sigma
Deployment, Seagate Technology

"Subir Chowdhury is one of the best of the 'new age' of organizational consultants. He has done a fantastic job of explaining a powerful concept in a simple and entertaining way."

—Marshall Goldsmith, Executive Director,
Financial Times Knowledge Dialogue

"An entertaining and profound introduction for the non-statistician! *The Power of Six Sigma* leaves readers inspired, wanting to learn more and get involved. Management guru Subir Chowdhury has made a superb contribution."

—Michael George, Chairman, George Group

"Subir Chowdhury provides us with a clear message as to the impact Six Sigma can make on any business. He explains how these disciplined, customer-focused processes enhance organizational effectiveness and provide bottom line results. In a highly competitive, chaotic world, predictability is achieved through the Six Sigma system as described in this book."

—Stuart R. Levine, Chairman and CEO, Stuart Levine
& Associates LLC, Former CEO, Dale Carnegie
and Associates, Inc.

". . . is an excellent overview that demystifies the key elements of implementing Six Sigma. Subir Chowdhury has provided an enlightened summary of the critical success factors required for understanding the power of Six Sigma. A must-read for executives and managers who are considering this management philosophy for their organizations."

—Dick Smith, Partner, Six Sigma Consulting,
PricewaterhouseCoopers

"Six Sigma has become a central part of business success, and everyone must know and apply these principles to their organization. *The Power of Six Sigma* will promote buy-in within all levels of the organization, as it breaks down what can be a complicated topic into an easy-to-understand, enjoyable read. This book will become a sourcecode for those who want to understand and execute Six Sigma successfully."

—Dave Ulrich, Professor of Business,
University of Michigan

DEDICATION

To the memory of Dr. W. Edwards Deming
and
To all the men and women who embrace
QUALITY in everything they do

CONTENTS

PREFACE

When General Electric CEO Jack Welch started singing the praises of a new management strategy called Six Sigma, Fortune 500 companies around the world began adopting the program—often before they knew what they were getting into. As a result, not all of those companies could duplicate the results that GE, Allied Signal, and others have achieved, despite spending millions on the program. This has been especially disappointing for the CEOs who made optimistic estimates of future savings to shareholders.

I have visited some of these companies, talked with their CEOs and strategists, their quality professionals, and their assembly line workers. The program is supposed to drive out fear, but I saw fear alive and well and in everyone's blood. And that is why I decided to write this book.

This book is for the CEOs who write huge checks to consulting firms without knowing what Six Sigma really is or how it works. It's for the strategists who have not yet fully grasped how improved quality can beef up the bottom line. It's for the middle managers who have to follow the boss's orders without believing in the program. But most of all, it's for the "rest of us": the line workers, support staff, and others in nonmanagerial positions who fear yet another program coming down the pike and what it might mean to us and our jobs. This book will help us all—and in the process, help our respective companies achieve the goals only Six Sigma can help us reach.

My hope is that *The Power of Six Sigma* will simplify what can be a complicated, intimidating subject in a lively, entertaining style—a style unmatched by any of the many other books on the topic. It makes Six Sigma accessible to everyone from Silicon Valley entrepreneurs to restaurant managers, from multinational CEOs to assembly line workers. *The Power of Six Sigma* is not a how-to book, but an introduction to a management strategy that is transforming the corporate landscape—and maybe beyond.

As I finished this manuscript, the most powerful nation in the world was going through a turbulent time in which it had not yet picked its next leader a month after the election. I couldn't help but hope that the nation's leaders would read this book to avoid the mistakes and waste that led to that fiasco. As you and hopefully thousands of readers will soon discover, *The Power of Six Sigma* could have helped!

Subir Chowdhury
Executive Vice President, ASI–American
    Supplier Institute
E-mail: subir@amsup.com
<www.amsup.com>

MOVING DAY

I held the cardboard box in my hands. I stared at all the things on my desk, and sighed. I tried to think of something neutral, something soothing, something to calm my soul, but all I could come up with was, "Never thought it would come to this." It didn't take. I could still feel my pulse throbbing in my fingertips, my eyes burning, my feet frozen in place as if made of lead.

I had never felt so blindsided, so humiliated, so stupid for not seeing it coming. But could I have seen it coming? I threw this onto the growing pile of questions for which I had no ability or energy to answer that morning.

To avoid falling into that abyss further, I returned to the mechanical task of packing up my books, my files—the ones *they* let me keep after pulling those *they* felt might contain privileged information—and the framed photos of my wife and kids into the box.

When I looked at the photos, I felt another stab of emotion pierce my heart. How was I going to tell them the company had let me go? Better question: How will they respond? What will Kelly say? What will she think of me? Will she stay? I always assumed she would, but then it always seemed like such a remote possibility that I never really thought it through. I guess I'll find out now.

Other questions kept bubbling up to the surface against my wishes: What would I do next? What kind of job can a 40-something manager get after being canned? How long will it take to find one? Will we have to move? Will the family move with me? And, how are we going to pay the bills in the meantime? Geez, we've got a bloated mortgage and two car payments, and we're trying to save some money for the kids' college tuition and maybe a nice vacation each year. Oh man. What a mess!

I came to, and realized I hadn't moved a muscle in—what?—a minute or two? More? I had gone almost catatonic. It was all too much. When I looked around, I saw the security guard at my door staring at me, trying to figure out if I was okay. I tried to reassure him with some sort of smile, but I couldn't muster anything better than a wiggly half-frown, which probably concerned him even more.

My friends in the department were just as uncomfortable. They wouldn't even stop by my office to say good-bye, instead they sort of scooted past the window, trying to get a quick look and move on. Drive-by glancers. Maybe they feared they might catch this mysterious "disease" if they shook my hand.

In fairness, they probably didn't know what to say. And to be honest, I don't know what I could have said to them, either. My eyes were welling up, threatening to erupt. A word or two from a co-worker— former co-worker, I corrected myself—might have been enough to start me bawling uncontrollably right there in my office. Maybe they sensed that. Even the security guard at the door had taken to staring at his feet, unable to watch me complete my final task.

I stared at the photos for a time, then finally placed them carefully in the box. I set aside my dark thoughts of home and office and returned to the slow task of packing up my things.

When I picked up my nameplate, however, I held it and whispered the words to myself: "Joe Meter, Manager, American Burger." I remembered the pride I felt on my promotion to manager eight years ago, overseeing 60 franchises in my region. Eight years ago? Had it been that long ago? Another stab. The future had looked so bright. I figured the promotion to regional manager was just a holding station. Didn't know it would be my last stop. I laid the placard gently at the bottom of the box.

"Not your fault, Joe," I thought, trying to reassure myself. "Nobody wants to eat burgers anymore. It's Southwestern nowadays, it's Asian; it's who-knows-what-else coming down the pike, but it's not burgers."

So why was I getting the shaft? When some corporate consultant told me this morning that they were letting me go, he tried to buffer the news by telling me they were letting a lot of guys go—but why me? Why not Jones in the office next door? The guy had only been a manager for a year, for crying out loud!

What had I done to deserve this? I didn't make waves, I didn't play games with sick days, I didn't even fiddle with my expense reports—and *everybody* was doing that!

My anger consumed me for a minute or two—my fists clenched in rage—before exhausting me. I slumped back in my chair, legs splayed, arms hanging over the side. I looked awful, but what did I care? What were they going to do—fire me? The security guard took a step toward me, perhaps fearing that I'd had a heart attack, before I waved him off.

It was only 11 o'clock. Getting called into the boss's office, being told I would no longer be needed at American Foods because our division just wasn't cutting it, then hammering out the details of my departure—it was already a full day. I felt worn out. I had no idea how I was going to spend the rest of the day, with nothing to do until my wife, Kelly, and our kids, Jack and Jane, got home. Go for a long walk in the woods? Lie on the couch? Nothing held much appeal—my thoughts threatening to invade any peace I might try to achieve.

As I finished cleaning out my desk, I discovered a stack of old business cards I'd tucked away in a drawer. I was about to throw them out because they were a few years old, but I stopped myself when I realized I might be needing one of those contacts to get my next job. I flipped through the cards, one by one, trying to remember who these people were. Few rang any bells.

I finally came upon Larry Hogan's card. Hogan, my old buddy from the mailroom. We started out together 20 years ago, a couple of college kids jamming envelopes into boxes while carrying on a running dialogue about all the characters and blowhards we'd met in the hallways. And about our dreams.

We talked about how we'd change American Foods if we ran the show. American Foods started in the 1950s as a wholesaler to fast-food joints, until the owners realized they could open up their own fast-food places. That's how American Burger got its start in the early 1960s, followed by American Chicken and American Sandwich in the early 1970s, and the fledgling American Pizza in the late 1980s.

American Foods, though, still produces the supplies for the restaurants, everything from the lettuce to the grills to the silly hats the clerks have to wear.

Larry and I called our game "King of the Forest." "Okay," we'd say, "if you were King of the Forest, what would you do about so-and-so?" We shared a lot of ideas—commonsense ideas, most of which, in hindsight, probably would have worked—but half the time the answer was simply, "Fire 'em! Cut the fat! Get rid of the deadwood!" I winced again. I wondered what the 20-something me would say about the 40-something me? I didn't have the energy to contemplate that. Another day.

> *We shared a lot of ideas–commonsense ideas, most of which, in hindsight, probably would have worked–but half the time the answer was simply, "Fire 'em! Cut the fat! Get rid of the deadwood!"*

I stared at the card. Last I saw Larry, five years ago, he was on the pizza side of the company. Whenever we saw each other, we'd always find ourselves talking about the old days. Seems like you have a special bond with the people you meet when you are young, a bond that no other friendships can match. Before I thought it through, I found myself dialing the number on the card.

When the phone started to ring, I woke up from my trance. What was I thinking? I hadn't talked to this guy in five years! And what was I going to say? "Hey, guess who just got canned?" What did I want from him, anyway? Maybe, in hindsight, I just wanted to talk to someone who might understand what I was going through before I went home. But before I could think it all the way through, someone picked up.

The woman who answered said, "Yes, Mr. Hogan still works here, but he's moved up to an executive position. May I ask who's calling?"

I hesitated, until I saw the security guard looking at me warily. "It's Joe Meter," I said. "An old friend."

"Okay, Mr. Meter. Let me see if Mr. Hogan's in."

While I waited, I pondered what she'd told me. An executive, huh? Well, that just goes to show you, I thought, I should have gotten in on the pizza side. Then I wondered if he would take my call. The last thing I needed, I realized, was any additional humiliation. Why did I expose myself to this? I was about to fake a response—"Okay, just tell him I called"— for the security guard's benefit and hang up, when the receptionist broke in.

"Mr. Meter?" she said.

"Yes?"

"Mr. Hogan is on the line."

"Hey old buddy!" he exclaimed, giving me more than I expected. "Kinda busy right now"—my heart sank—"but my lunch appointment just canceled. I know it's short notice, but any chance you can meet me for lunch?"

I breathed a sigh of relief. "As a matter of fact, I'm unexpectedly free, too."

LUNCH IS SERVED

An hour later I was driving to have lunch with an old friend from the mailroom. Larry picked one of the new company restaurants, of course—an American Pizza store. Although I really didn't feel like going to a company store, where I might run into someone I knew, I didn't want to tell Larry why I felt that way. No point telling him right off the bat that I'd just gotten the axe.

The restaurant had just opened a few weeks ago, so I wasn't prepared for what I saw: pizza makers spinning the dough in the windows, a greeter meeting me as soon as I walked in, and such a clean, well-lit place. Opening their own sit-down restaurants was American Pizza's latest project.

I had no trouble recognizing Larry. Of course, with all the restaurant employees calling out "Hello, Larry!" he would have been hard to miss. Sure, he had aged a bit since I had last seen him five years ago. He had lost a little off the top, added a little around the middle, and had a few more wrinkles—probably from grinning so often. But he still looked strong and vigorous, with a ready smile and a sparkle in his eyes. The world had not beaten him down, as it seemed to have done to so many of my old colleagues—me included, I had to admit.

Larry perked up when he saw me, shook my hand vigorously, and said, "Great to hear from you, Joe! Thanks for coming out on such short notice," he added, apparently unaware that my daily schedule was suddenly quite open.

"How's the family, Larry?" I asked.

His wife, Renee, and his daughters, Emily and Kate, were all doing fine, he said, but since both kids were in junior high, he'd succumbed to buying a second phone line for them upstairs. "Occupational hazard, I guess," he joked. "So how are you?"

"Okay," I mumbled.

"Family doing fine?"

"Yes, yes," I said, snapping out of it. My two kids had just entered high school and were both playing basketball, I told him, and Kelly's career in real estate was taking off. I didn't tell him that she's already paying more than half the bills—and might be paying all of them, for a while.

But when he asked how things were going at American Burger, I didn't see much point in snowing him. "Actually, I was laid off," I said, although I felt like I'd been fired, not released with a decent severance package. Still, I wanted to put the best face on it I could and keep a stiff upper lip. The last thing I wanted here was an emotional outburst. I composed myself and continued. "It happened this morning. They cleaned house."

"Oh no," he said, stopping in his tracks. "I'm really sorry to hear that, Joe. From the burger side?"

"Yeah," I said. "You know, I've been there since I left the mailroom."

"Ah yes," Larry said. Mercifully, he didn't dwell too much on it. "I knew the new American Foods CEO was going to make some cuts in that division," he said, giving me an out, "so I know you're not alone."

> **L**arry was doing his best to be nice about it but it didn't change things much. It doesn't matter how rare or common the disease is. If you've got it, that's all that matters.

Larry was doing his best to be nice about it, but it didn't change things much. It doesn't matter how rare or common the disease is. *If* you've got it, that's all that matters. But it was nice to hear a sympathetic voice, something I didn't hear from anyone when I was packing up my things. It was also nice to be pampered by the greeters, who took our coats and gave us numbers without looking for a tip, and to have our seats pulled out for us by the hostess. Small gestures go a long way on days like this.

"Well, what about you?" I asked, settling into my seat. "Executive? That's a big step up from the mailroom!"

"I suppose so," he said. "Hey, as I remember it, you got the first promotion out of the mailroom!"

Another painful flashback. What had happened? Without intending to, Larry proceeded to answer my question. "You know, in hindsight, being left behind was probably a lucky break for me," he said, "although it certainly didn't feel that way at the time! Geez, was I jealous of you. Fifteen years ago burgers were selling like, well, burgers. You had the most burger stands in the country—4,000! And American Pizza was just a start-up with a few dozen shops. But I got lucky."

"I'll say. Who knew that burgers would dive, and pizza would skyrocket?"

"Well, yeah, I guess," Larry said. "But that's not what I meant. I got lucky because shortly after I moved over to pizza, Cathy Baker became head of the pizza division."

"The Queen of American Foods?" I said, and we laughed again, chuckling over Baker's recent business magazine cover, which identified her as one of the most powerful women in business and even used her office nickname. "What'd the story say, the brains behind American Pizza?"

"That's her," Larry confirmed. "You've got to give her credit. She was bold, willing to take a chance. What the heck, we only had 5 percent of the market anyway."

"I remember," I said. "You guys were barely on the map, while we had over 50 percent of the burger market."

"Hey, sometimes it *helps* to have nothing to lose!" he joked.

"Don't I know it," I mumbled, finding just a little humor in my new situation for the first time.

"You'll be back on your feet before you know it," Larry said, and I think he meant it, although I found it pretty difficult to believe at that point. I almost objected to the comment, but I felt his intentions were good and let it slide. "Anyway, Cathy got us started on this new program called Six Sigma," he said.

"Sick Sigmund?"

> **"S***ix Sigma–the number six, and sigma, the Greek letter. But Six Sigma means something more in business and industry. It represents a statistical measure and a management philosophy."*

Larry chuckled. "No, Six Sigma. The number six, and sigma, the Greek letter. But the expression 'Six Sigma' means something more in business and industry. It represents a statistical measure and a management philosophy."

Just then the waitress arrived at our table. Larry said, "Hello, Susan. How are you today?"

"Just fine, Mr. Hogan," she said. "Nice to have you back."

"Nice to be back," he replied. "Susan, this is an old friend of mine, Joe Meter. Make sure he gets the VIP treatment, wouldja?"

"But of course, Mr. Hogan!" They chuckled. Turns out their motto is, "*Everyone* gets the VIP treatment at American Pizza."

Looking at the menu, I was stunned by the number of salads, appetizers, and entrees. They'd definitely expanded their repertoire. Nonetheless, at Larry's suggestion I decided to try their New York thin crust pizza, with barbecued chicken and tomato. He got a mini-deep dish, and we were back to talking.

"Well, what's so great about Six Sigma?"

Larry grinned. "Glad you asked."

SWALLOWING SIX SIGMA

"Whenever anyone hears 'Six Sigma,' they flinch," Larry admitted. "They think it's going to be really complicated, or something forced on them by the boss. But it's really a pretty simple system. It gives people well-defined roles and a clear structure to their tasks. It works best when everyone's involved, from the CEO at the top of the organization to the guy in the mailroom—like our old jobs. In fact, the guys who run Six Sigma projects are usually in the middle of the organization."

> **"S**ix Sigma works best when everyone's involved, from the CEO at the top of the organization to the guy in the mailroom," Larry said.

He looked at me, then said, "Joe, I can't help but notice you're already folding your arms."

I looked down—he was right—and we both smiled.

"Heard it all before, haven't you?" Larry guessed, correctly.

"Afraid so," I said. That was one plus to being fired anyway: I didn't have any more incentive to fake excitement for the next management initiative. The last thing I needed on this day was to listen to another one. But Larry was a nice guy and a sympathetic soul with nothing to gain from pitching this new idea, so I decided to hear him out. Besides, the alternative was to go home, alone, and wait for my family to return and tell them the news. And that thought chilled me. So, I mustered what little enthusiasm I had for Larry's idea, and said, "Well, what's it all about?"

"The real power of Six Sigma is simple," Larry said, "because it combines *People Power* with *Process Power*. Still skeptical?" he asked. I grinned, confirming his suspicion. "Well, let me walk you through it and see what you think."

"Okay," I said, giving Larry my patented show-me look. "Good luck."

> **"T**he real power of Six Sigma is simple," Larry said, "because it combines **People Power** *with* **Process Power."**

"Here goes," he said, undaunted. "In football, you've got two ways to win games. The first is making more spectacular plays, like long passes and big runs and great interceptions. That's the stuff that makes the highlight films. But you can also win games by making fewer mistakes: fewer penalties, fewer fumbles, fewer interceptions. It might not be as spectacular as all the big plays, but it's just as important to the bottom line. And the thing is, while you need spectacular players to make spectacular plays, *anyone* and *everyone* can focus on making fewer mistakes.

> **"G**ood companies focus on not making mistakes: not wasting time or materials, not making errors in production or service delivery, not getting sloppy in doing what they do best."

"Companies are the same way. They can make more money by coming up with great inventions, hiring away some real stars, or buying other companies. This stuff makes the headlines. But good companies also focus on not making mistakes: not wasting time or materials, not making errors in production or service delivery, not getting sloppy in doing what they do best. It may not be as flashy as inventing the Palm Pilot or buying up a competitor, but it's just as important.

"Preventing mistakes can make you just as much money, or more, and anyone can do it. Everyone can help the company this way—and themselves, too. When you head up a Six Sigma project, you get a lot of authority, a lot of recognition, and, most importantly, the support you need to succeed with your project. To top it off, most companies sweeten the deal by giving the project leaders, and sometimes the entire team, a financial reward for pulling it off. Could be stock options or a simple bonus or a percentage of the money saved on each project. Depending on the company, it can run anywhere from 2 or 3 percent all the way up to 20 percent. But trust me, even a few percent can add up pretty quickly. Most give the leaders a percentage—say 2 to 5 percent—of the money saved. When you realize that the average Six Sigma project saves about $230,000, you can see how quickly the money can add up. Just do the math."

"How about *you* do it!" I said, grinning.

"Works out to a bonus of from $4,000 to $10,000," he said, "although the projects can vary quite a bit. With me so far?"

"So far," I said, willing to concede only that much. When I worked at American Burger, I'd been trained in a dozen or so programs. They all started out sounding like the Great Unifying Theory of Business, only to be reduced to just another improvement initiative thrown on top of the growing pile. I didn't have much stomach for more. "But you know," I said, finally speaking up, "we've been through a lot of these things, and if we'd done all the things we were supposed to, American Burger would still be going strong—and I'd still have a job."

"Touché, my good man," Larry said. "But hear me out. I think you'll be convinced, when you hear how it works, that this one's different. After all, you've seen how American Pizza's grown from a few dozen stores to a few thousand."

"Fair enough," I said. "For an old friend, I'll listen."

"Six Sigma is a management philosophy focused on eliminating mistakes, waste, and rework," he said. "It's not a rah-rah 'Do Better' program. It establishes a measurable status to achieve and embodies a strategic problem-solving method to increase customer satisfaction and dramatically enhance the bottom line. It teaches employees how to improve the way they do business, scientifically and fundamentally, and how to maintain their new performance level. It gives you discipline, structure, and a foundation for solid decision making based on simple statistics. It also maximizes your return on investment and your Return on Talent™—your people."

"It all sounds good, Larry," I said. "But to be honest, *all* these programs *sound* good."

"I can see your point," Larry said. "Been through a few initiatives myself. But I'm convinced this is the best thing we've seen in a long time. And if you're the same guy I remember with all those common-sense solutions in the mailroom years ago, I think you'll be convinced, too—if you give it a chance. Ask any question you want."

"Alright," I said, not knowing enough about it to even ask a very insightful question. I started with the most basic question—really, the only question I could think of. "What does Six Sigma mean, anyhow?"

"Popular question," Larry said. "But it's nothing to get stuck on. Sigma is just a Greek letter that looks like an 'o' with a slight hook at the top—kind of like a sideways 'Q.' It is used to designate a standard deviation."

I didn't care to confess that I really didn't know what standard deviation was or how it worked. I think Larry sensed this. But before he could say anything, our food arrived—about ten minutes after we ordered it. I wanted to ask how they got it here so fast during the lunch rush, but I decided to let it wait until Larry was done.

Seeing my blank expression, Larry clarified his point.

"If you want to get technical about it, *standard deviation* is a measure of variation within a process."

"Example?"

"Let's say you have a thermostat, and you're trying to keep your room temperature at 70 degrees. The thermostat is supposed to perform within 67 to 73 degrees, which we can refer to as *requirements*. In reality, the thermostat fluctuation is between 68 and 72. That's a pretty small amount of variation compared to the requirements; so the thermostat's performance is acceptable in that case. But, if the temperature is bouncing back and forth between 55 and 85 degrees, that variation does not meet the requirements. This means the performance of the thermostat is unacceptable when compared to the requirements."

"I'd say," I offered, happy for the chance to recover.

"Sigma is like a measurement, used to determine how good or bad the performance of a process is; in other words, how many mistakes a company makes, doing whatever it does."

"So, *Sigma* is like a measurement, used to determine how good or bad the performance of a process is; in other words, how many mistakes a company makes, doing whatever it does, from manufacturing steel to delivering the morning paper.

"The thing is," Larry continued, "we measure the performance of different things every day without even thinking about it. Every time you walk into your corner store, for example, you're measuring the quality of the selection, organization, and service of the store against the 'norm' you've established from previous visits. If the store is out of your favorite soda three visits in a row, or the place is a mess, or the clerk is rude, you're going to take mental note of that. And if it keeps up, you're going to conclude that the performance of the store falls far short of meeting your expectations or requirements—it's too inconsistent—and take your business elsewhere."

"Alright," I said. "What does the *Six* mean?"

"It's the Sigma level of perfection we're shooting for," Larry said.

> "*What* does the Six mean?" I asked.
> "It's the Sigma level of perfection we're shooting for," Larry said.

"Explain," I said.

"Well, let's say your company's working at One Sigma. That means it's making about 700,000 defects per million opportunities, or DPMO."

"Not too good," I ventured.

"No, not too good at all," Larry chuckled. "At One Sigma you're only doing things right 30 percent of the time. Two Sigma is better. If you're working at Two Sigma, you're making a little over 300,000 mistakes per million opportunities. Most companies operate between Three and Four Sigma, which means they make between approximately 67,000 and 6,000 mistakes per million chances, respectively. If you're operating at 3.8 Sigma, that means you're getting it right 99 percent of the time."

"Well, you can't do any better than that," I replied, trying to sound knowledgable.

"Most folks would agree with you," Larry said. "But it turns out even a 1 percent margin of error can add up to a lot of mistakes pretty fast. Getting it right 99 percent of the time is the equivalent of 20,000 lost articles of mail every hour. It's 5,000 botched surgical procedures every week. It's four accidents per day at major airports!"

"I see what you mean," I said—and for once, I meant it. "I think our average store screwed up only a dozen or so burgers a day."

"But don't you see?" Larry asked. "A dozen bad burgers a day creates a dozen lost customers for life, not to mention the poisonous word of mouth. You know the stats: 1 happy customer tells 3 people, 1 unhappy customer tells 20. That's 240 people who heard about those botched burgers!"

"When I started out at American Pizza," Larry continued, with a sympathetic smile, "if we were going along at 3.8 Sigma, that would mean about two ruined pizzas a night—and we ruined a lot more than that! In reality, we probably ruined more like a dozen or so, which works out to about Three Sigma. But after we adopted the Six Sigma approach, we've gotten up to a Five Sigma. We've virtually eliminated bad pizzas, and now we're mopping up other error zones. So, you see what I'm talking about."

"I do," I said, chomping into my New York style thin crust pizza. "And by the way, I have to admit this pizza is pretty good."

"You like it, eh?" Larry asked, visibly pleased. "That's a new one we're trying out. Hopefully, you're not alone."

"Back to Six Sigma," I said. "Everybody wants to improve quality. We hear it all the time. But just coming up with a number to achieve perfection doesn't make it happen."

"No," Larry said, "But it's a start!

"Think about it; when you go on a diet, do you say, 'I'm gonna lose some weight until I look good,' and hope for the best? Or do you say, 'I'm at 200 right now, and I'm getting down to 180, and that's that'?"

I nodded. He had a point.

"If you want to improve something, you have to know where you stand and where you want to go, or else it isn't going to happen. But when you define those things in anything but numbers, the goal quickly becomes subjective and fuzzy. Numbers bring clarity.

"Trying to improve something without having a goal—a *numerical* goal—is like trying to lose weight without having a scale," Larry explained. "Six Sigma people often say, 'If you can't express what you're trying to say in numbers, you probably don't know what you're talking about.' Everything in Six Sigma can be measured, and that's how you figure out what to fix and when you've actually fixed it. Dreams don't come true, Joe. Goals do. It's all manageable when you write it down."

"**I**f you want to improve something, you have to know where you stand and where you want to go, or else it isn't going to happen…. Numbers bring clarity."

"Makes sense," I had to admit, stopping my eating just for a moment. "So the whole idea of Six Sigma is to improve quality?"

"Well, actually," Larry said, grinning, "that's probably the most common misconception, that the be-all and end-all of Six Sigma is to improve quality. But in Six Sigma, improved quality is a means to an end, not the end itself. The goal is not simply to improve quality for the sake of improving quality, but to make customers happier and add money to the bottom line. If you're improving quality but still upsetting customers or losing money, you're missing the point."

I mulled over the many quality programs we had embarked on that did just that: missed the point. A lot of them screamed about how crucial it was to improve quality and customer service, but they never connected those things directly to profits. They seemed to teach us to win the battle but lose the war by putting all our time and money into customer satisfaction while raising costs. Well, here was my chance to put it to Larry. "Improving quality costs money, Larry, which is why we often lost money on the other programs. How can you possibly improve quality *and* save money?"

"That's the *second* most common misconception!" Larry said with a laugh. "You're good!

"You see, most companies think improving quality costs money, so it's a trade-off, a tug-of-war between your customers and your accountants. They ask themselves, How much quality can we *afford* to give the customers and still make a profit? But Six Sigma companies flip that. They've learned that

> **"S**ix Sigma companies learned that quality saves money, because there are fewer throw-outs, fewer warranty payouts, and fewer refunds. And doing all that, in turn, increases profits."

quality *saves* money, because there are fewer throw-outs, fewer warranty payouts, and fewer refunds. And doing all that, in turn, increases profits.

"You and I both know that senior management almost always has a love affair with the finance department and the bottom line. Six Sigma marks the first time that finance and quality have been put on the same team, working together, not against each other. Now senior management sees that quality *helps* the bottom line, so they believe in it.

"And for some reason," he added, "I don't think the guys at American Burger ever saw it that way."

No kidding, I thought, but there wasn't much point in blasting my former employer at this point.

"But then, I guess, few do," Larry assured me. "It's amazing, how much money we spend to attract customers, and how little we do to keep them after we've got them. You only have so much pull on a guy who's never been to your store, but the guy already *in* your store—geez, we've got to keep that guy. He's already taken the bait! All we have to do is exactly what we say we will in our advertisements: give him an excellent product and excellent service at an excellent price. Keep *that* guy—and get his friends—and you don't need to advertise nearly as much. At American Pizza, we decided to focus on customer *retention.*"

I didn't have the nerve to mention just how much we had spent on ads, promos, and the like at American Burger just to get customers in the door—I knew it was in the millions—and how little we had spent on keeping them happy after they came through our doors. Unfortunately, all of Larry's insights were coming a day late for me. But there had to be more to Six Sigma than just a number, or just the goal of retaining customers. I mustered my cynicism to ask a few more pointed questions.

"But we're all human, Larry," I objected. "We're going to make mistakes. How do you squeeze more perfection out of us without making us miserable? You can only crack the whip so many times before we get tired and discouraged."

"Another good question," Larry said. "I'll tell you how it works."

"Hey, I'm not going anywhere," I said, belying more bitterness than I wanted to. I didn't want Larry to feel sorry for me. I regained my composure. "Honestly, Larry, everyone tries to minimize waste, to eliminate mistakes. What's so new about that?"

"Well, nothing's new about that, obviously," he said. "But the *way* Six Sigma addresses those issues —*that's* what's new. It's not just a quality initiative, it's a *management philosophy* that covers a lot more than just defect rates."

"Try me," I said, the skeptic inside me alive and well.

Larry laughed at my cynicism. "You asked for it."

As the waitress cleared our table, we settled in for a deeper discussion over some fresh gourmet coffee.

THE CRUCIAL
DIFFERENCES

"How many different manage-ment initiatives did you have to endure at American Burger?" Larry asked.

"Ah, geez," I said, shaking my head. "Well, let's see. There was Total Quality Management, or TQM. That was okay, as far as it went. There was ISO 9000, which helped us document our work but didn't seem to help much toward improving product or process quality. There were probably a few more, but I just can't remember any more."

"You've blissfully forgotten them, right?"

"Guess so," I said. I was a little reassured to know that Larry wasn't just a rah-rah manager, on board for whatever his bosses fed him. He'd grown as tired of the steady stream of programs as I had.

"Quality programs seem to come down the pike every few years," he said, "whether they help or not. But this one's really different."

"What's so different about it?" I asked.

"Well, a lot of quality programs boil down to glorified pep talks," Larry said, "where you just try to motivate the employees to do better."

"Been around that block before," I said.

"Haven't we all?" Larry replied. "Most of the other approaches you've mentioned try to promote continual improvement, but they aren't very systematic. They're sort of like, 'Hey, can you see if you can do your job a little better, please?' Imagine a football coach whose whole game plan consisted of yelling, 'Work harder! Play better! Good luck!' without telling you what to do or giving you the help you need to do it!"

I couldn't help but chuckle at that. Apparently, we'd both had plenty of bosses who fit that bill.

"Some of the better ones still focus only on the end product," he added, "where they spend all their time trying new ways to identify the bad 'biscuits' you've already made and make sure they get thrown out before they get to the customers. That will help you to a point, of course. It might get you to about Three or Four Sigma."

"But Four Sigma still leaves the dreaded 1 percent rate of error, right?"

"Good memory!"

"Well, how do you get rid of that 1 percent?" I said, sipping a little more hot coffee so Susan could freshen it up a bit.

"For starters," Larry said, "instead of just getting rid of the bad end products, you try to solve WHY the bad results are occurring. In the case of a biscuit factory, while other programs tell you to oil the machine and toss out the burnt biscuits, Six Sigma tells you to take the whole machine apart, find out why it's making the occasional burnt biscuit, fix the problem, then put it back together again so you don't have any more burnt biscuits. That way, you don't need a dozen Quality Control guys with clipboards standing there at the end of the line watching the biscuits drop into the out box!" He added a little sugar to his coffee and continued.

"There's no point throwing good money after bad, which is what a lot of programs seem to recommend. They urge you to keep driving a horse with a bad leg to make it go faster. Better to fix the leg or get a new horse. Why keep oiling a machine that makes bad biscuits? Break it down and put it back together, or get a new machine that doesn't have the same defect. Don't keep patching leaks. Build a better boat! Don't keep paying for constant tune-ups on a car with a rotten engine. FIX THE ENGINE!

"Six Sigma doesn't try to *manage* the problem, Joe. It tries to *eliminate* it."

It all seemed so simple, I thought, that I couldn't help but wonder why *we* didn't think of it in the burger division. But I wasn't giving up that easily. "Okay," I said, warming to the challenge. "How do you figure out what the problem is in the first place?"

Larry answered my question with a question. "Think about it, Joe. What's the goal of Six Sigma?"

"To improve—no, wait," I said, catching myself. I remembered that quality improvement was the means to the end but not the end itself. I had learned over the years how to play the game and learned new lingo each time a new program came along. I quoted the mantra: "To make customers happier and increase profits."

"Very good!" Larry exclaimed, parroting a school teacher's delivery. "Now, who determines what to do to make customers happier and increase profits? The executives, the accountants?"

"All of the above?" I offered.

"Actually, we ask the *customers* what problems we need to solve. If we correctly identify and solve those problems, we'll save money and they'll be happier. Fact is, what *we* think the problem is might not be what the *customers* think it is—and their opinions are more important than ours on that stuff."

"For example?" I asked.

"Okay, let's say I work for a carmaker, and sales are sluggish. Now, being a car buff, I might conclude sales are down because our car doesn't have enough power, so I recommend pouring millions of dollars into researching and building a stronger engine, adding $1,000 to the sticker price. But then I'm stunned when sales slump even lower. Reason? The customers didn't care about the engine. It had plenty of driving power. All the customer really wanted was a better cup holder. We could've done that for five bucks, saved a ton of money, and sold more cars! *That's* how you can increase customer satisfaction and save money in the process: Ask them what they want and give it to them!"

"Sounds like our American Deluxe," I said, referring to a headline-grabbing blunder we created a few years ago. It was right up there with New Coke and Pepsi Clear, the butt of stand-up comics' jokes for months. "We convinced ourselves that's what people wanted—a jazzed-up burger with Dijon mustard—mainly, I think, because that's what *we* wanted. But they didn't have to eat American Burger every day in their cafeteria. *We* did. Turns out what *they* really wanted was just the same old cheeseburger we'd been making, but two minutes faster than we were making it at the time, in a cleaner store, with friendlier service. Somehow we didn't see all that."

"How'd you learn all that?" Larry asked, surprised. "You guys had that kind of market research going?"

"No," I said, grinning sheepishly. "Read it in a magazine. *They* did the research that we probably should have done."

"Hm. Well, at least *someone* was reading the magazine!" Larry laughed and patted me on the back. "We've all made the same mistake, Joe: assuming what we want is what the customer wants. That's why it's so important to *start* with the customer and work your way *back* to the *source* of the problem."

Funny, just getting a pat on the back from Larry made me feel a little better. It'd been a long time since I'd gotten any positive feedback, no matter how small the gesture, from anyone at work. Larry's employees, I thought, must feel lucky—and I felt a little envious. "Anyway," I said, "You've talked to your customers, and you've identified some problems. Then what?"

"Well," he said, "the first thing you *don't* do is try to save the world—just a corner of your business. Once you have the data telling you what customers want, and what you can do better, the tendency is to try to fix everything at once—and that never works. You end up wasting time and money and frustrating everyone—including the customer—while doing nothing very well. In Six Sigma, you pick *one* problem to solve at a time as a project. You'd be amazed how much difference that can make."

"Fine," I said. "But which one do you pick?"

"The one you think is going to produce the biggest bang for the buck," he said. "The juiciest, lowest-lying fruit you can find. Go for the biggest cost-guzzling problem you have—the one that has the most room for improvement and will yield the greatest savings and customer satisfaction. Then you put someone in charge of the project."

"An executive?"

"Not usually, no," Larry said. "Usually someone in the middle, someone we call a 'Black Belt.'"

I couldn't help but laugh. My cynicism was back. "A Black Belt?" I cracked. "And do you play *Kung Fu Fighting* whenever he walks into the room?"

We both laughed. "I know, I know," he said. "But don't tell that to a Black Belt! They take a lot of pride in what they do. Unlike TQM and other programs, where everyone's supposed to turn things around in their spare time, the Black Belt only has one job: to complete the project given to him. And he also gets all the help he needs from the Champion—his supervisor—and the Green Belts—his support staff."

"Whoa, whoa, whoa!" I said. "Hold the phone right there, Larry. Where are all these guys coming from? Black Belts and Green Belts and Champions, oh my! Did you guys turn your division into a playhouse or a martial arts studio? Got a bunch of Power Rangers or Ninja Turtles coming out next?"

Larry enjoyed a good-natured chuckle. "I know, I know," he said. "The titles definitely sound silly at first. But once you see what all the roles do, you see them differently."

"Give it a shot," I said with my cocksure grin intact and my arms folded once more.

PEOPLE POWER
Who Does What

"One of the most important elements of Six Sigma is the role everyone plays," he said. "This is the *People Power* side of the equation. Any good football coach will tell you the same thing: Every player must have a specific role, clearly defined, with consequences for not coming through and rewards for doing their particular job well. And that goes for everyone, from the quarterback to the waterboy."

"Alright," I said. "But what *are* those roles?"

"Okay, it breaks down like this," Larry said. "Starting at the top . . ."

"Of course," I said. "Classic top-down enforcement."

"Not so fast," Larry countered. "The projects are run by the Black Belts in the middle. But if they're not *supported* by the top leaders, you know and I know that project is not going anywhere."

I conceded the point with a nod.

"If the top dogs don't take the time to learn about Six Sigma or support it, the project leaders don't stand a chance," he continued. "Any project without that kind of backing is a project that's set up for failure."

"I've been put in charge of a few of those," I mumbled, my resentment of being thrown to the wolves momentarily overcoming my skepticism of Six Sigma. Nothing burned me more than to knock myself out for the latest initiative, only to discover that the guys who'd assigned it didn't care or notice if I'd come through or not.

"Almost everyone's been put in that position, my friend," Larry said. "And no one goes away feeling good about it, either. The top brass feel like the programs are a waste of time and money, the project leader feels like he's been left to twist in the wind—or worse, set up as the fall guy—and the customers don't receive any benefit at all. All they notice are higher prices and a demoralized, fatigued service staff."

Bingo, bingo, and bingo, I thought. But I wasn't yet convinced that Six Sigma could prevent all that.

"Okay," I agreed. "So what do the players do?"

"Again, starting at the top," he said, pausing to wink at me to get the okay to proceed. I nodded. "You've got to have the Executive Leadership on board, the same way you have to get the owner of a football team on board. The Executive Leadership has to be the driving force behind adopting the Six Sigma philosophy and inspiring the organization from Day One. If the leadership isn't ready to do what's necessary to win, the team won't. Likewise, if the CEO and his or her minions aren't behind it, or don't understand how it works, it won't fly. But if they get it, and back it, everyone else will get the green light to make a go of it. And let me tell you, no one is a bigger cheerleader for Six Sigma than Jack Welch, the CEO of General Electric, who got the idea from Lawrence Bossidy, Allied Signal's former CEO. When Bossidy filled in for Welch at a GE management meeting, he explained how Six Sigma transformed his company and inspired all of Welch's executives to do the same.

"The Executive Leadership has to be the driving force behind adopting the Six Sigma philosophy and inspiring the organization from Day One."

"Bossidy's 70,000 employees make fibers, plastics, and aerospace and automotive parts—you name it. And Bossidy applied Six Sigma to every one of their business processes, from inventing and commercializing a new product to billing and collecting after they deliver the product. Six Sigma has improved Allied Signal's products, their price, their customer satisfaction, and—not least—their cash flow.

"Now you've got converts like Ford's Jacques Nasser, Caterpillar's Glen Barton, and a bunch of others following Bossidy's lead.

"In other words, Six Sigma is a lot bigger movement than what you see in our little old fast-food company. Six Sigma can be used in the service industry, manufacturing, operations—everything from steering columns to French fries.

> "*A good CEO will likely appoint one of his executives to oversee and support the entire mission. This sends the signal to everyone that the company is serious.*"

"But it starts at the top.

"A good CEO will likely appoint one of his executives to oversee and support the entire mission. This sends the signal to everyone else that the company is serious. It might be a vice president or a director of manufacturing or marketing, somebody who's highly visible and has pull. And that executive is called the Executive Champion."

"So we've gone from martial arts to a golf tournament?" I cracked.

"Very funny," Larry said, but with good humor.

"Okay, okay," I said, trying to stop laughing. "What does the Executive Champion do?"

"Well, he's sort of the general manager . . ."

"Oh, great!" I snorted. "Now we're playing football again?"

"Honestly," Larry said, "you're taking a lot of liberties with your . . . liberation."

"Sorry, sorry," I apologized. "Please, go on."

"So the Executive Champion acts as the general, picking his personnel with great care," Larry continued.

"And not just assigning the office deadweight to a dead-end task?" I interjected.

"Right," Larry said. "The people working on a Six Sigma project are usually the *most* valuable people in the corporation. When it's time for the Executive Champion to pick the Deployment Champions and the Project Champions, he or she picks from one of the highest levels of the corporation, for example."

> **"T**he Deployment Champions provide leadership and commitment and work to implement Six Sigma throughout their businesses," Larry said.

"But what do those guys *do?*"

"The Deployment Champions provide leadership and commitment and work to implement Six Sigma throughout their businesses," Larry said. "Project Champions oversee the Black Belts and their projects. They help the Black Belts by breaking down corporate barriers, creating support systems, and making sure money is available to get the job done. They also help the Black Belts pick their improvement projects, size up what the organization can do, and benchmark the organization's products and services. The bottom line is, the Project Champions pick, evaluate, and support the Black Belts in tackling their projects. They're the foundation for success, without which the whole thing is bound to fail. And that's why smart Executive Champions pick the cream of the crop to do these jobs."

Shifting gears, Larry asked, "Wanna hear a story?"

"Sure."

"When the CEO of a major conglomerate decided to introduce Six Sigma, he asked all of his managers to make a list of the people who might be able to replace them if they were to get sick or die suddenly. After the CEO had a brush with death, you understand, being replaced was on his mind. Anyway, the managers came back with lists of their top people—and the CEO turned around and tabbed these stars to run the Six Sigma projects. *That* told the managers, more than anything, that he was serious about it—and also helped ensure Six Sigma's success."

Interesting approach, I thought. On more than one occasion, I suspected the people picked for such assignments were the "least valuable" people at the office—and sometimes, I suspected, that person was me.

"Anyway, where was I?" Larry asked.

"Project Champions," I said, noncommittally.

> **"T**he Project Champion's job is to oversee, support, and fund the Six Sigma projects and personnel necessary to get the job done. This allows the people on the project to focus solely on the project at hand."

"Right! Thanks. The Project Champion's job is to oversee, support, and fund the Six Sigma projects and personnel necessary to get the job done. This allows the people on the project to focus solely on the project at hand."

"Good idea," I said. "I remember too many times getting an assignment from one guru, while still having to finish all my usual duties—and neither got done well. I felt pulled in both directions and was unsuccessful at both. Ultimately, I just put the assignment aside and returned to doing what I was paid for."

"Exactly!" Larry said. "That's what *almost always* happens with new initiatives. And, that's *exactly* why

55

we need Champions to clear the tracks for the project managers."

"And who are the project managers?" I asked. "The all-knowing gurus?"

"Good one," Larry said, grinning at my latest crack. "No, they're called Master Black Belts."

"Close!" I said, getting in another friendly shot. Larry let it pass with a wan smile. "Okay," I said, looking to make peace. "Who are the Master Black Belts?"

"When a company first decides to go with Six Sigma," Larry explained, "the role of Master Black Belts is played by outside consultants who come in to act as in-house experts on Six Sigma. That means they teach the core points of Six Sigma to Black Belt candidates throughout the company. At the top end, they help the Champions select good projects and the people to run them. Then they train and coach the people who will be doing the day-to-day work of Six Sigma and report the company's progress on the projects. The Master Black Belts are the people most responsible for creating lasting, fundamental changes in the way the company operates from top to bottom. To do all that, the Master Black Belts must have

> **"T**he Master Black Belts are the people most responsible for creating lasting, fundamental changes in the way the company operates from top to bottom."

the ability to pick the right projects and the right people, and teach, coach, and monitor them."

"That's a lot," I said.

"It is, which is why the outside consultants do the job at first," Larry said. "But when the people they've trained are ready, they take over the job of Master Black Belt from the consultants."

"Wait a second," I said, in disbelief. "You mean the consultants' job is to make themselves obsolete?"

"You got it!" Larry answered, with a chuckle.

"Wow," I said. "This *is* different."

"*Now* you see!" Larry said, pointing. "I've given you a lot," he added. "Let me sum it up: The Master Black Belt works with the Champions to pick the project they're going to work on and the people who are going to work on it. Then they train and coach those people to succeed. The most important person they pick, though, is the Black Belt."

"Ooooh, the Black Belt!" I joked.

"Hey, buddy, don't laugh," Larry said, playfully making a fist. "Being named a Black Belt is what got me out of the American Foods backwaters and onto the fast track."

"How did *that* help?" I asked, incredulous.

"The Black Belts are the people who really do the work," Larry explained. "They're the key to the whole project, the true leaders of Six Sigma. The biggest mistake a company can make is naming an employee who's not committed to be a Black Belt. That can virtually guarantee the failure of Six Sigma."

> "*The* Black Belts are the people who really do the work," Larry explained. "They're the key to the whole project, the true leaders of Six Sigma."

"So how does the Black Belt make it succeed?" I asked.

"Good question," Larry said. "First, you need to find people who have considerable intellect and drive and to be willing to think 'outside the box,' as we say—outside your usual way of thinking. Black Belts must have both management and technical skills—a mix not everyone possesses—and the ability to inspire passion in front-line employees and the confidence of the top brass. The biggest thing they do, though, is turn the Six Sigma vision into reality. They put the rubber to the road."

"Gotta be hard to find all that in one person," I said.

"You might think so," Larry countered. "And, obviously it's impossible to find the perfect Black Belt. But we did find that we had a whole pool of talented folks waiting to be recognized, looking for an opportunity to test themselves and make a difference—a much bigger pool than we expected, frankly. Turns out talented, ambitious people don't like spending their careers in second gear. Who knew?" Larry joked, palms up.

I grinned, but I couldn't help but think of myself when he said that.

"Once they're picked, the Black Belts have to dive in, take the bull by the horns, and . . ."

"Come up with more cliches?"

He laughed. "Yeah, that too. They have to know when to hold 'em, when to fold 'em, when to walk away, and when to run. Joking aside, there's some truth to that. They help get funding for the project, so they have to decide where to put their resources. Executive Leaders and Champions worry about *what* gets done, while Master Black Belts and Black Belts focus on *how* things get done. And in the process, they strive to achieve goals they never thought possible. But they are possible. A new Black Belt can save the company $150,000 to $175,000 per project. Multiply that by four to six projects annually, and you're talking about savings from $600,000 to over $1 million a year."

"And before you know it," I mused, "you're talking about real money."

"You got that right," Larry said, smiling at the joke.

"So how do you find these superheroes?" I asked.

"Fortunately, we know a few things from our experience about where to look," he said. "We've learned it's helpful to find someone who's already familiar with the company but may be frustrated by the company's old approach. Managers with a technical background seem to do better than others, too. Having said that, rookies can sometime bring a boldness to the project that goes a long way. If you have the numbers, a mix of the two is often quite effective, for obvious reasons."

"How long does the typical Black Belt serve?" I asked. "And don't tell me, It depends."

Larry grinned. "Well, it *does* depend," he said, raising his finger to stop my interrupting, "but generally Black Belts are most effective when they're in the role for at least two years but not more than three."

"Thank you for the surprisingly straight answer," I said. "Okay, the next obvious question: After you've picked the best candidates for Black Belts, how do you *train* these superheroes?"

"Very carefully," Larry replied. "The training lasts four weeks . . ."

"Four weeks!" I blurted out. "Sounds like a lot!"

"Relax!" Larry said. "This won't hurt a bit."

"I'm sure!" I said. "Think I've heard that before!"

Larry laughed. "I should have explained that after each week of training, the Black Belts go back to the workplace and put into practice what they just learned."

"Wouldn't it be faster just to have them take all four weeks of training in succession?"

"Faster, but less effective," he said. "An old proverb says 'Tell me, I forget. Show me, I remember. Involve me, I understand.' When people get to practice what they've learned, it sinks in better. They get it. This way, they can see it work, and they don't become brain-dead through nonstop training. And they start saving the company money immediately, because they're already trying out what they've learned on their first project."

"Okay," I said. "But what DO they learn?"

"Oh, LOTS of things," Larry answered. "There are four core phases of the training, which match the four main points of the Six Sigma strategy: how to Measure, Analyze, Improve, and Control the processes that produce increased customer satisfaction, company savings, and a healthier bottom line. These four phases are composed of things like statistics, quantitative benchmarking, and design of experiments."

"But don't most managers already know those things?"

"Some know some of it, of course, but almost no one knows all of it," Larry said. "More importantly, few know how to apply all of it to Six Sigma projects. How many training courses have you attended over the years?"

"Ah, geez," I said. "Two dozen—maybe more?"

"And what happened?"

"You sit down for a few days, while someone at the front of the room fills your head with a bunch of ideas—most of it either obvious or incomprehensible. Then you go back to your job, a few days behind, but no smarter."

"Sounds about right," Larry said. "We call those kinds of courses Data Dumps. The guy just unloads his overheads on you and doesn't know or care if it sinks in, or if you *get it*. But with Six Sigma, like I said, you break the Black Belt training down into four parts, and after each training session, you go back and *apply* what you've learned. That way, you remember it, but you also have a lot more incentive to learn when you're in class.

"You know," he added, "we had a real struggle at American Pizza getting guys motivated for Six Sigma at first . . ."

"You don't say!" I exclaimed. "Hey, you know and I know that a week of class for a new program is everyone's worst nightmare."

"True enough," Larry conceded. "We got past that by asking the guys, So, are you ready to start the first step of your Six Sigma project right now? Then they ask, What was that first step again?" We both chuckled. "When they *know* they're going to apply what they learn a week later and are accountable for it, that changes everything. They *want* to learn; they *want* the help. And once they're in class, they realize Six Sigma teaches some familiar topics in unfamiliar ways. Everything is geared to be applied specifically for Six Sigma."

Larry explained that the future Black Belts spend one week on the first subject, How to Measure, then return to the workplace to try out what they've learned on a *specific project* before coming back for the second week of class to learn the second subject, and so on. Think about it: If you're taking golf lessons or piano lessons or any kind of lessons, the instructor doesn't give you a solid week of lessons and then expect you to have mastered the craft. They generally give you one hour of instruction, let you practice for a week, then come back to learn the next step. That's how Black Belt training works, too.

"I think you can appreciate by now why the Black Belt is the most important link in the chain."

"And not the top dog—or what was it, the Executive Champion?"

"Nope. Like I said, we need their support, but it's the guy in the middle who makes the whole thing spin."

"Well, you've told me what the Black Belts do," I said, "but not necessarily *why* they're more important." Fact is, I was surprised that anybody would give a middle manager that kind of responsibility, that kind of power.

"The Black Belts and the Master Black Belts are the *only* people in the chain who work *full-time* on the Six Sigma project and *only* the Six Sigma project," Larry said. "Remember, the Executives and the

Champions might decide *what* gets done, but it's the Master Black Belts and Black Belts . . ."

"Who figures out *how* to get it done," I said. "I *do* remember. But why would they give a middle manager that much authority?"

"Simple," Larry said. "It's like General Patton said: 'Never tell people *how* to do things. Tell them *what* you want done and they will surprise you with their ingenuity in getting there.' In other words, the more authority you *give* them, the more creativity and energy you *get* out of them. If something's your baby, and you'll get the credit or blame for it, trust me, you'll work a lot harder. If you're just a member of a committee and no one's really in control or accountable for the group's success or failure, don't expect much from that group.

> *"Never tell people how to do things. Tell them what you want done and they will surprise you with their ingenuity in getting there."*

"But the biggest things a Black Belt gets are *structure* and *tools,*" Larry added. "The structure is to know what to do and when, with deadlines and numerical goals in place, and the statistical tools are for analyzing how you're doing and what needs to be done next."

"Sounds like a lot of pressure," I countered.

"In some ways, maybe," Larry said. "But being a Black Belt also gives you a lot of visibility, a lot of credibility. It makes it fun to come to work when you've got so much power and responsibility."

I couldn't remember the last time it seemed fun to go to work in the morning. Seemed like my job consisted mainly of a lot of pointless, anonymous busywork, with no end in sight. I had to admit, I would have taken on more responsibility if it came with some excitement.

"Another thing we've found," Larry added, "is that people seem to *like* the structure, the plan of attack, the numerical goals, and the specific roles that Six Sigma offers. I know I did!

"I once taught a seminar on the coast," he continued, "and asked the 20 participants how many of them had bosses who truly valued them and wouldn't

THE POWER OF SIX SIGMA

want to lose them. Only *one* raised her hand!" Larry said. "You know, in all my years at American Foods, the biggest complaint I've heard from dissatisfied employees is not low pay, long hours, or a hectic schedule. It's this: 'I don't know what my boss wants,' and 'No one appreciates what I do.'"

"Here, here!" I said, and Larry patted me on the back again.

"Well, Six Sigma eliminates a lot of that," he said, "because there's no question as to what's expected of you, when, and why. And because of all that accountability, there's no mistaking just what every member of the team has accomplished when a project is completed."

"So is that it?" I asked. "Executive Leaders, Champions, and Black Belts? Sounds like the Black Belts have to do an awful lot on their own."

"Not quite," Larry said. "That's where the Green Belts come in."

"Green Belts?" I asked. "A friend of mine in a martial arts program got a green belt as soon as he joined. The black belt indicates mastery, I guess, but I think the green belt indicates that your check has cleared. Apparently, it's awarded for good credit."

We both laughed at that one. "Well," Larry said, "in Six Sigma, it means a little more than that. The Green Belts provide the Black Belts the support they need to get the project done."

"The worker bees," I said.

"Yeah, sort of," Larry said. "But they're trained in Six Sigma, so everyone is speaking the same language and is working for the same goals. That's the power of Six Sigma: It's the first management philosophy that runs top to bottom, so everyone's on the same page.

> **"T**he Green Belts provide the Black Belts the support they need to get the project done."

"And unlike the worker bees," Larry continued, "the Green Belts can work themselves up to Black Belts if they do well."

"Who decides that?"

"The Black Belts themselves, who train the Green Belts and direct their efforts."

"Well, what happens to the Black Belts when the Green Belts get promoted?"

"The best ones move up to Master Black Belts," Larry said. "And the best of those move up to Champions and eventually Executives. In fact, Jack Welch himself told his employees at GE straight up that if they wanted to get promoted, they'd better be Black Belts."

"Promises, promises," I said, with a friendly grin.

"Hey, it worked for me," Larry said, arms out. "I wasn't going anywhere at American Pizza until they made me a Black Belt."

"Well, what did you *do?*" I asked. "How long does the average project take?"

"Usually, about four to six months," Larry said. It was refreshing to get a concrete answer, instead of the tired, "It depends on a lot of factors" routine.

"Where did all this come from?" I found myself asking. "Who came up with this idea?"

"The Six Sigma philosophy has been around for a while, actually," Larry said. "A few guys at Motorola came up with the concept in the mid-80s, tinkered with it, and are now spreading the word to other companies."

"Like who?"

"You name it," Larry said. "The Six Sigma list of devotees reads like a who's who of the Fortune 500: General Electric, Allied Signal, Sony, Motorola, and Polaroid, among others. But the biggest early convert, though, was undoubtedly General Electric's CEO Jack Welch. In 1995, GE's operating margin was about 13.5 percent. By 1998, it was up to 16.7 percent, a number Welch previously thought was impossible. That represents a $600 million bonus to the bottom line."

"Hmmm," I said.

"You probably can understand," Larry concluded, "why Welch himself called Six Sigma 'The most important initiative GE has ever undertaken.'"

PUTTING PEOPLE POWER INTO PRACTICE

When I took a moment to look around, I noticed most of the lunchtime crowd had left, but Susan hadn't forgotten us. We were never treated like malingerers.

If Six Sigma is so powerful, I began to wonder, why hadn't we heard of it at American Burger? "When did *you* hear about Six Sigma?" I asked Larry.

"About ten years ago, not long after I moved out of the mailroom to American Pizza," Larry said. "When I first got there, we were last in our field and built to stay that way. We really weren't doing much right, it seemed to me, and we didn't have much motivation to do things better. To be perfectly honest, I didn't know what American Foods was doing in the pizza business in the first place."

"We probably got into the pizza business because everyone else was," I offered. "Seemed like the thing to do, would be my guess. Besides, we had lots of money to burn at that time from the burger side of the business."

"True enough," Larry said. "And we burned it! Those stores were financial blackholes, and we kept making it worse by pouring money into every crazy idea going around the country—fancy delivery cars, new uniforms every year, and one ad campaign after another that usually contradicted the one immediately preceding it.

"But everything changed for us when Cathy Baker took over. She got us off the ground. First meeting, she told us we were going to turn things around and become a force in the field. At the time, we figured the boss was nuts. When we were given free pizza for our breaks, hardly any of us would eat it because we burned them so often.

"But Baker said we had to start by asking a lot of new questions about how we do business and take nothing for granted. I still preach that. I tell my people that simply saying, Hey, we've done it this way for 20 years, is just not a good enough answer. Twenty years ago, we weren't even on the radar! Twenty years ago, almost no one was on the Internet or had a cell phone. Things have changed!"

"No kidding," I said, dolefully. "Twenty years ago, we *owned* the burger market."

"True," Larry said, but he was nice enough not to rub it in. "The point is, things change, and we have to change, too. Cathy told us we had to let go of some bad habits. One of them was ignoring customers and the employees who serve them. *They* see and hear things guys in the office don't. They know why a machine malfunctions; they know why customers are upset. They also know how to fix the darn machine and make the customer happy again—if we give them what they need to do the job."

"So, what were the answers?" I asked. Sometimes my ignorance, I realized, was impossible to hide. At American Burger, I don't think anyone had any idea what the customer wanted. We certainly never asked.

The mysterious demise of American Burger was becoming less mysterious each minute I listened to Larry. "What *did* the customers want?"

"Once Cathy committed to Six Sigma, we started to find out," Larry said. "One of the first things she did was pick several of us for the job of Black Belt."

"Were you excited?" I asked.

"Hardly!" Larry protested. "I thought it was the kiss of death! And for good reason. You remember how these things used to go. When the top brass jammed a new quality program down your throat, you tried to pick someone you could afford to miss for a few weeks to run the show."

I laughed. I'd been on both sides of that equation—the dumper and the dumpee. Neither was much fun. I remembered how we all hoped to be overlooked for such exalted posts.

"And on top of all that, I was a 30-year-old buck, the assistant manager for one of the stores," Larry added. "I certainly didn't have any reason to think I'd be tabbed for greatness! Why would they pick *me* to run a program they really cared about?"

"What changed your mind?"

"Cathy called me into her office and explained to me exactly what was going on," Larry said. "She told me that our division was in deep trouble, which I knew, and that Six Sigma might save us, which I doubted!

"She also told me that the entire organization was committed to this, including the top brass, or Executive Leadership, as we call it. And she was also on board, the Deployment Champion. She told me she'd studied the program carefully and even conducted a fairly lengthy search for people to run some of the most critical projects, the Black Belts. It was nice to hear, but I figured it was just flattery, until she told me that they were going to give me a four-week training program, spread out over four months, at a cost of about $15,000 to the division. But in exchange for all that, she expected me to help American Pizza save $250,000. Now, all *that* got my attention!"

I was leaning forward now. He was drawing me into this thing. "So what happened next?" I asked.

"Okay, so I went to the Six Sigma training," he said, "and learned about how to measure things, what to measure, and what to do with those num-

> **"S**he told me that they were going to give me a four-week training program, spread out over four months, at a cost of about $15,000 to the division. But in exchange for all that, she expected me to help American Pizza save $250,000. Now, all that got my attention!"

bers. They got me looking at things in a completely different way."

"How so?"

"Ready for the breakdown?" he asked.

"I'm ready for the breakdown," I said, shaking two fists in mock enthusiasm.

PROCESS POWER
The Five Steps of Six Sigma

"This is the *Process Power* part of the equation," he said. "Goes like this: The first step is to DEFINE what the problems are . . ."

"Where the shoe pinches," I interjected.

"Exactly," he said. "But the key is to focus not simply on the *outcome,* which almost everyone does, but on the *process* that creates the product or service. Then, *map* that process so you can easily recognize the links between the steps! Sometimes *that's* where the problems are—not in the teeth, but in the gaps between the teeth."

"So the goal is not only to brush, but also to floss."

"Hey, not bad!" Larry said. "Mind if I steal that one?"

"Be my guest," I offered magnanimously.

"Another key: Don't just complain about things that can't be fixed, like the weather. Focus on problems that you *can* fix. There's no point cursing the darkness, as they say. It's not a bitch session. The key is to define the problems *objectively* . . ."

"Numerically?"

"Bingo! If we say, 'Our quality is inconsistent,' or 'Customers don't like the New York–style pizza,' what does that mean? How do you make quality *more* consistent or fix the darn New York–style pizza with data like that? The more accurately you define the problem, the more precise your target, the better your chances are for hitting the bull's-eye.

"When you gather data on the problem, you have to do it carefully, because you're writing the instruction booklet for the rest of the project. Do a sloppy job here, and your chances for success are as slim as your chances for programming your VCR correctly the first time using those awful instruction books.

"If you go to the doctor and just say, 'I don't feel good,' and he doesn't ask more questions or conduct any tests, he's probably not going to get too far in trying to make you feel better. Clarity, clarity, clarity! And it starts with clearly identifying the problem.

"Think about it," he continued, clearly on a roll. "When effective armies go to war, they don't say, 'See if you can drop a bomb somewhere in enemy territory.' They say, 'Attack the military base, not the bakery, and it's located at these coordinates.' Then, you know exactly where to strike!

"And you know, it's interesting. Somehow, just soliciting the problems from your customers and employees makes them feel better—because someone's finally listening to them—and the act of writing the problems down makes them feel more manageable. Instead of an ill-defined gray cloud hanging over your company, your problems become clear, specific items you can identify and correct. It's reassuring to see that problems can be broken down, listed, and attacked. Instead of just looking down at your belly and saying, 'Boy, am I out of shape,' you look at a cold, clear number indicating how much you weigh and write down another number indicating where you want to go. Suddenly, it doesn't seem so impossible."

"So, you list all the problems you've got . . ." I said, getting him back on point.

"As many as you think are necessary," Larry corrected. "Starting with what the customers think, then go onto what the guys think who deal directly with the customer or with the machines that create the product."

"Okay," I said. "Then what?"

"Pick the problem that's giving you the most trouble, the one that's costing the company the most, the one that's making customers unhappy—the one that will reward you the most if you can fix it," Larry said. "We're not looking for carpet-bombing here but a surgical strike. Bombing the bakery might deprive the citizens of a few jelly donuts, but it won't get at the core of the problem. You need to attack the shipyard.

"In our business, if we want to get the pizza to the customer faster, we don't bother trying to speed up our delivery cars," he explained. "Sure, they might save an extra second or two on acceleration when the light turns green, but for the money it would cost us, it'd hardly be worth it. If we focus instead on speeding up the cooking process, then we're onto a more cost-effective solution."

> **"P**ick the problem that's giving you the most trouble, the one that's costing the company the most, the one that's making customers unhappy–the one that will reward you the most if you can fix it," Larry said.

"Makes sense," I said. "So, you've got the problem."

"Then you go onto the second step," he said. "You MEASURE."

"Measure what?" I asked.

"Lots of things," Larry said. "Let's go back to the doctor's office for a minute. When you say you don't feel good, a good doctor won't just say, 'Okay, let's run these tests,' because she'd have no idea which tests to run and would waste a lot of time and money going down blind alleys. Instead, she'll ask you where it hurts, when it hurts, and a bunch of follow-up questions, so she can begin to narrow down the possibilities. Only *then* does she start running tests.

"Likewise," Larry continued, "once you've got the right tests set up, it's time to measure the *capability* of a given process—what's possible—by measuring how many opportunities for defects a certain process or operation presents. In baseball terms, it'd be equivalent to keeping track of how many chances for errors a fielder has—how many fly balls or grounders come his way. From there the Black Belt calculates how many errors are made, which is called the frequency of defects.

"Put the second number over the first," Larry explained, "and you've got your fielding percentage. Most companies measure the number of *errors,* but not the number of *opportunities,* so they don't know what's possible, and how far they're falling short.

"Next, do some *benchmarking* by measuring the competition's fielding percentage on that problem," he said. "How are they doing on the same problem you've picked? How does that compare to your company's performance? Before most companies start breaking it down by the numbers, they usually assume they're one of the best in the field for quality, efficiency, and customer satisfaction. And why not? They've usually been in business for a while—and for good reason. But after they look around and compare what the competition's doing, they usually discover that they're not as exceptional as they thought.

"Lawrence Bossidy, the former Allied Signal CEO I mentioned earlier, tells his staff they should assume that every one of Allied's competitors does at least one thing better than Allied. After all, they must be doing *something* right, or they wouldn't be in business.

"The concept's pretty simple. If you're a pro golfer and you want to improve, you break down your game piece by piece. How well do you drive, how well do you chip, how well do you putt? Then, compare your numbers to the best driver, the best chipper, the best putter. How do you measure up? And most importantly, what is the best golfer in each area doing that you're not? Doesn't matter if their *overall* score is better than yours, only if they can teach you something in one part of the game."

I nodded.

"Let's say our problem is consistency," Larry said. "Let's find out who has the best consistency in the business—or even observe companies in another field if that helps. Benchmarking tells us what's possible and gives us a reasonable goal. Then, we figure out what they're doing that we're not.

"During the entire measurement process," he added, "it's important for the Black Belt to focus on the 'critical to quality,' or CTQ, characteristics— those that have the most impact on the outcome. For example, a team's players may not be very tall compared to another team's, but that fact may not be critical to quality. How they field ground balls, however, surely will be. So, the Black Belt needs to find out which elements are critical to quality."

I was no Black Belt, of course, but it wasn't hard to understand that figuring out which elements were critical to quality—in this case, catching and throwing the ball—was vital to improving your fielding.

"Of all the steps to Six Sigma," Larry said, "the *measurement* phase is probably the most underestimated, in terms of its importance and the time and money it takes to do it right. Because it's not that flashy a step, and nothing really *happens* in measurement, there's a tendency to zip through it without much thought. But that's a big mistake, because good numerical data is the foundation for Six Sigma. Without good data, you can't make good decisions. There's an old carpenter's maxim: If you think it will take one day and a hundred bucks, plan for two days and two hundred bucks. The same is true on measurement."

"I'm with you," I said. "So you've got all this data. What's next?"

"If the data's good," he said, "you can start the next step: ANALYZE the numbers to find out how well or poorly the processes are working, compared to what's possible and to what the competition's doing. Done right, the first three steps will show you the maximum results possible if everything is perfect, and also how far your company is falling short. If the gap between the two isn't great, you don't have much to gain from improving your performance, so move on to the next problem. If the gap *is* great, start digging in. You're onto something valuable.

"The big questions to answer, of course, are *why* the errors are being committed and *how* to fix them. Is it poor technique fielding fly balls, bad throwing arms, or not enough range to field ground balls? If you set the experiment up right, the numbers will tell you the answers. If you don't get the numbers you need, go back to the drawing board and set up a new experiment—the same way a doctor would order more tests."

> **"T**he big questions to answer, of course, are why *the errors are being committed and* how *to fix them."*

"Sounds great," I said, "but what are you looking for? How do you know when you've hit paydirt?"

"If you can answer when, where, and how often the defects occur, you have what you need," Larry said. "But don't just focus on the symptoms of the problem. Find the *root causes*. If you stop looking for the problem halfway, you'll come up with a half-baked solution to eradicate it."

"Let's say we play by the rules," I postulate. "We identify a juicy problem, we measure how we're doing, and analyze the numbers. What do we do with them?"

"You decide how far off the mark the numbers are," Larry answered. "Once you know what you really weigh, you decide what your target weight is and put together a plan of attack to get there, including a diet, exercise program, and deadline."

"But a business just *ain't* that simple," I said.

"True enough," Larry replied. "That's why the Six Sigma classes teach statistical reasoning, among other topics, to help the Black Belts compile and use the data in the most effective way possible. Responding to that data is the next step: IMPROVE the processes you're pursuing."

"What's the pitch?" I asked. "Are we back to, Hey, everyone, could you please do your jobs better?"

"No, it's more sophisticated than that—thank God!" Larry laughed. "Since we've already identified which CTQ components are not meeting our expectations, we then focus on implementing changes that will improve the specific CTQs. This will improve the whole process. Let's say we've figured out, for example, that fielding is essential to winning baseball games, and that handling ground balls is essential to fielding well—and further, that we could do a lot better at that phase of the game. Then, it stands to reason that if we improve our ability to field ground balls, our fielding percentage will go up, and our winning percentage will follow.

"In business terms, you sit down with the data and your analysis and determine what's possible—what's a reasonable goal for this or that process. After you've established *numerical* standards, you calculate which of your 'tolerance bands' need to be tightened to get there and then how to go about tightening them.

"In the case of the baseball team, let's say we're winning an average of 80 games a year, but we've determined that with our personnel and facilities and budget, we should be able to win 90. To do so, we'll need to bring our fielding average up from 85 percent to 95 percent. And, to do that, we'll need to field 90 out of 100 ground balls successfully, not just the 75 we currently are fielding without errors. Now, how do we do that? Bring in a fielding coach to work on the techniques we lack. That coach—the Black Belt—figures out *specifically* what we can be doing better to field more ground balls cleanly—nuts-and-bolts things like bending our knees and keeping our gloves down on the ground."

"It's a long way from 'Please try harder,'" I said.

"Glad you agree," Larry said.

"So is that it?" I asked.

"Not quite," he answered. "It's kind of like losing weight . . ."

"Back to weight loss, eh?"

"Just for a moment. A lot of programs help a lot of people take off the weight, but the hard part is *keeping* it off."

"Don't I know it!" I said, patting my paunch.

"Exactly," Larry said, patting his in a show of brotherhood. "The last step is CONTROL, in which you lock in your successes."

"And how do you do that?"

"The Black Belts implement measures to keep the key variables within their new operating limits month after month," Larry said. "In this step, though, it's important to distinguish between statistical process *monitoring* and statistical process *control.* It's the difference between hopping on the scale every morning to *check* your weight and watching your calories each day to *control* your weight."

"I know the difference too well," I admitted.

"Don't we all," he said with a resigned grin. "Once the plan's in place, it's the Master Black Belt's job to make sure the team monitors the process, measures the results, and confirms that the plan is working. He or she also has to monitor variables that might be affecting the data, things they never thought about on the drawing board. If any new problems arise, they refine the process and reload.

"Long story short," Larry said, "you Define the problem, Measure where you stand, Analyze where the problem starts, Improve the situation, and Control the new process to confirm that it's fixed—DMAIC, or Dumb Managers Always Ignore Customers."

"Feel like I'm playing the piano again," I said.

"Sorry, buddy," Larry said. "But after my training, I had to score 80 percent or better on the final test to be certified as a Black Belt. You do everything you can to remember the information."

> **"L**ong story short," Larry said, "you Define the problem, Measure where you stand, Analyze where the problem starts, Improve the situation, and Control the new process to confirm that it's fixed–DMAIC, or Dumb Managers Always Ignore Customers."

"Hey, don't tell me where you got the matches," I said. "Just tell me how big the fire was!"

Larry had a good laugh at his own expense. "Point well taken, my friend," he said. "But the upshot is pretty simple. We measure what we care about. If we didn't value home runs, we wouldn't count them. Do we count foul balls? We start to measure it, we begin to improve our performance on it.

"Second, stick a date to everything you do. Without deadlines, it just doesn't get done. If the IRS said, 'Hey, just get your taxes in when it's convenient for you,' what do you think would happen?

"And third, assign very specific jobs to everyone on your team. That eliminates the confusion and lack of direction we talked about earlier, and also guarantees that the job gets done. Even the Red Cross advises rescuers on the scene to point to a specific member in the crowd to get a blanket, to another to call 911, and so on. Otherwise, everyone just stands there.

"Finally, put it all in writing and pass it around. If everyone can see who's doing what and when, that breeds some accountability."

PUTTING PROCESS POWER INTO PRACTICE

"So that's the theory," I said. "That's all fine and dandy, but when you get back from Six Sigma college, how do you put it into practice?"

"Oh, sure, bring reality into it!" Larry cracked. "After we asked our customers—the ones we hadn't already driven away—what they liked and didn't like about American Pizza, we sat down and looked at the numbers. Now, I would have guessed that they wanted more topping choices or more styles of pizza—deep dish, thin crust, and so on. But that's why we ask the *customers.*

"They didn't care about those things. What drove them nuts about us, it turned out, was burnt crusts. We decided to look into it, because it didn't seem like too hard a problem to solve, but one that would go a long way toward eliminating waste and pleasing the customers.

"The first thing we discovered was that we had to redefine our terms," he said.

"What, 'burnt' was too technical?" I said, chuckling.

"Actually, it wasn't specific enough," he said. "To us, a burnt pizza was one where the cheese had turned brown—or even black—forcing us to throw it out. To the customer, a burnt pizza was any pizza with blackened crust, anywhere on it. They were a lot more sensitive to it than we were. By *our* definition, we were burning about two or three pizzas per hundred, which isn't great, as we know now, but we thought it was pretty good at the time. That was about what the average American Pizza store was burning, and we threw the bad ones out. But by the *customer's* definition of *burnt,* we were ruining more like a dozen pizzas per hundred—and we were delivering them! We had a problem!

"When we started to look into it, we focused not just on the *outcome,* but on the *process* that produced it. We studied the stores—and more importantly, we talked with the employees who made the pizzas—and we wrote down the cooking procedure we observed and the chefs' complaints. Well, at the time, the poor chefs had to answer the phones, take down customers' orders and directions, and handle walk-in customers, all the while making and baking the pizzas. Right there, we knew, we had a recipe for disaster.

"Making matters worse, when it came time to pop the pizzas into the oven, these guys had to follow a ridiculously arcane system," Larry said. "They had to open the 600-degree ovens, which could fit three rows of three pizzas each, and use those big metal paddles to shuffle them around inside the oven as they cooked. They would move all the pizzas already in there toward the front, put the new pizzas in the back, then open it up a minute or two later to pull out the oldest pizzas, which were then in the front row, and add the newest ones to the back.

"Now, a pizza left alone in one of those ovens would be finished in about 8 minutes—actually about 7 minutes in the back, the hottest part of the oven, and about 9 minutes in the front, the coolest," Larry explained. "But each time they opened the oven to put a new one in or get an old one out, the temperature dropped 50 to 100 degrees, adding 30 to 60 seconds to the finish time of the pizzas inside. Do that four or five times in the average cycle of one pizza, and the 8-minute completion time was suddenly up to 12 minutes.

"On top of that, every time the chef stuck his arm in those deep but narrow ovens, he risked burning himself. We discovered almost 10 percent of our chefs got medical care and/or sick leave during the course of an average year. That represented a substantial cost in missed time and health care, not to mention a drain on morale and an increase in turnover, all of which cost money.

"But what we were looking for, of course, were burnt pizzas. Well, needless to say, you've got this crazy, inexact juggling system going on in the ovens, as well as dealing with the phones, walk-ins, and drivers—it's no accident that one in ten pizzas had some blackened crust. Given the system we had in place, we were surprised we weren't burning a whole lot *more* than just a couple dozen each night."

"So, you've got the problem, and you figured out why," I said, playing detective. "How'd you solve it?"

"At first we tried to fix the problem as we found it," Larry said. "By measuring the oven time of each pizza, we figured the finish times were all out of whack. So, we installed a rack of nine timers on all the ovens to keep track of how long each pizza had been cooking. It helped some—it got us down to about eight burnt pizzas per day per store—but it also resulted in bells going off all the time and didn't make the chef's job any easier, really.

"We went back to the drawing board and decided to pull the weed up by the roots," he said. "We concluded that so long as the chef had to keep opening and closing the oven to shuffle the pizzas around, the process was doomed to fail. We gave it some thought, asked everyone from marketing to manufacturing to throw their two cents in, and knocked some ideas around. We looked into giving each store another oven, hiring more chefs, or creating special clocks to stick on top of each pizza itself, but nothing was going to get the job done. We also looked into more quality control measures, but most of them simply helped us throw out more of the bad ones. They didn't help us avoid *making* the bad ones."

"Just throwing out the bad biscuits," I said, catching on a bit.

"Exactly," he said. "We decided the old system was just that—an old system not capable of meeting the current demand—and completely scrapped it."

"Man!" I said, unable to restrain my surprise. "*That* must've taken some guts."

"Under the old bosses, it would've been suicidal," Larry said. "But with Cathy pumping Six Sigma, it was a piece of cake. Remember, the job of the Deployment Champion is to give the Black Belt all the time, personnel, and money he or she needs to fix the problem. When I showed them our numbers, our observations, and our ideas—with the huge potential savings and earnings underlined—the bosses gave the go-ahead."

I was surprised—and pleased—to learn that, for once, upper management actually backed up its promise to support the initiative it had called for.

"Before we spent the money, though, we sat down with the appropriate people to get their thoughts on the issue. We laid out the problem, gave them our data, and told them what we were looking for. Together, we came up with a bold solution: We designed a conveyor-belt oven, where the chefs make a pizza, put it on a very slow conveyer belt, and watch it go in the oven. Each pizza comes out perfectly every time, seven minutes later. That machine has virtually eliminated burnt pizza at American Pizza. We still make the occasional one due to human error, but we've gotten good enough to do away with a lot of the after-production safeguards we had relied on to make sure we didn't deliver the bad pizzas. The chefs just don't have to worry about it."

"Well, great," I said. "But the machines must've cost a fortune!"

Larry quickly corrected this notion. "Not so," he said. "We were buying the old ovens from a supplier, who was making a profit on the purchase and the occasional service and parts they required. We had about 2,000 stores at the time, so it added up. Since we designed the conveyor ovens ourselves—and kept them very simple—we actually saved money on the ovens and their upkeep. Plus, we saved untold thousands by not having to buy back or remake ruined pizzas. And we were even able to reduce our chef staff slightly—for a month! After that, our demand grew because we could promise the perfect pizza . . ."

"The Perfect Pizza Promise," I said. "I remember those ads."

"Guess they worked!" Larry joked. "So we didn't have to lay anyone off, although we *did* manage to reduce the ratio of chefs per pizza made."

"Quite a success story," I said. Hey, it was impossible not to give the guy *some* credit.

WE DELIVER

"Once we'd finished that project, I figured that was it, I'd be back to my old job as assistant store manager. But Cathy was so impressed, she told me to tackle another problem. We decided to zap the next most obvious bug. Again, we went to the customer and the frontline employees, and they told us that since we'd fixed the burnt crust problem, their biggest problem was not getting the pizza there on time—and sometimes not at all.

"They had a point," Larry offered, with a wink. "After all, it doesn't matter how good the pizza is if you never see it. But once again, if we hadn't asked them, we would've thrown a ton of money into things the customer just didn't care about.

"Once again, we had to check our terms and make sure we were measuring the right thing. What is a *botched delivery*? To us, it was whenever the right pizza didn't get to the right house. We felt if we made a mistake but eventually fixed it, that was still a successful mission. By our count, we were getting it right 97 percent of the time, which is about 3.4 Sigma. But to the customers, a botched delivery occurred whenever they received anything less than a perfect pizza the first time, on time. By *their* definition, we were only getting it right 87 percent of the time! Not good enough!

"But we still had the problem: How to get the pizza to the customers on time, every time. We watched and talked to the workers in the stores and quantified what we saw and heard—and by the way, you have a lot more credibility with your people when you can back up what you say with numbers—and a few things emerged pretty quickly."

"Such as?"

"Such as the guy who took the customer's order was the same guy who was trying to make the last caller's pizza. They never had the time or know-how to repeat the customer's order or address back to the caller. I mean, how many times do *we* get lost driving around, because we don't take the time to get the directions right? Better to spend an extra few seconds on the phone, than a few minutes driving around the wrong neighborhood. If they needed to check an address, they only had an outdated phone book and a greasy paper map taped to the wall. They passed on this dubious information to the driver, who had no time to ask questions and no phone in the car for backup. Once again, when we started looking at the process, we were amazed we delivered *any* pizzas to the right house at the right time!"

"Agreed," I said. "But a conveyor oven isn't going to get you out of this one."

"True," Larry said. "This time we had to work with the people in human resources and sales and marketing to get a workable solution.

"Since I had the support of my Champion above and the Green Belts below," he continued, "I had the power to do what was necessary. I tested the waters. I had human resources experiment with hiring an extra employee *just* to answer the phones at each store. I installed computers in each store for the receptionist to punch in the customer's phone number and order. With just the phone number, that computer then beamed up all the customer's important information—name, address, directions, even a shortened purchase history. By clicking the mouse, the computer would spit out the information and mark the house on a half-page map, drawing in only the streets the driver needed. The customer's order, meanwhile, showed up on the screens the chefs read back in the kitchen.

"We also installed cell phones in all our cars. That way, if anything went wrong, the driver could call the store or the customer and get things fixed fast, before we had to make a new pizza."

"You really went hog-wild," I said. "How much did all that set you guys back?"

"Hey, by that time, we had some backing, we had some momentum, we had some guts!" Larry said.

"You also had some money!" I pointed out.

"True," Larry said, laughing. "But we'd already saved the company a nice pile. And, we brought in more cash by expanding our customer base. But once again, we didn't spend as much as you might think. Remember, I had to show that we'd be *saving* money. The computers, cell phones, and locators were all one-time expenditures, which we could buy in bulk. Second, the extra person we hired to answer the phones actually made the pizza makers *much* more efficient, so we could improve our chef-to-pizza ratio once again. And keep in mind, we were losing *thousands* every week on lost pizzas. So I had some money to play with."

"Did it work?"

"Like you wouldn't believe," Larry said. "We couldn't believe it. We were far more efficient, so we could make more pizzas at each store and deliver more pizzas on each driver's run. And because we weren't buying back or remaking a dozen or two pizzas a night, everything we took in, we kept. Needless to say, morale was sky-high, too. No one wants to work for a loser."

"So that was that?"

"Not even close!" Larry said. "By this time, I *preferred* running projects to running a store. I had power, I had responsibility, and I could see results! I was also getting a piece of the savings, too. And that made for a pretty sweet bonus for all the work I was doing.

"We then decided to work on human error—simply hearing the order incorrectly," he said. "With the help of human resources, we set up a straightforward training program that taught the receptionist how to punch the order and phone number in, repeat the order and the address back to the customer, and make sure they got it right. That cost peanuts and saved another one or two buybacks per night.

"Same strategy, same results: more efficient workers, fewer refunds, happier customers. We were heroes!"

> **"S**ame strategy, same results: more efficient workers, fewer refunds, happier customers. We were heroes!"

"*Then,* did you go back to your old job?"

"Nope! Cathy wanted more! So we took on a harder problem: failed stores. Our region had suffered too many failed stores, so we decided to find out why. We pulled in the finance guys to take a look, and they determined that our biggest problem was poor location, of course, followed by lack of floor space. We compared our strong and weak stores, and we discovered that the strongest ones were located next to large populations of single men. Think about it: Who buys the most pizza?"

"Bachelors!" I guessed.

"Right-o!" Larry said. "So, we revised our real estate policy, setting up our largest shops next to college campuses, military bases, and factories. It worked! We knocked our dropout rate down to 2 percent, and the change barely cost us a dime.

"Hey, you just see a ghost?" he asked.

I was flabbergasted and apparently looked it. We had almost all of the same problems American Pizza had, but we hadn't done any of this stuff—hadn't even thought of it—and it all seemed so simple in hindsight.

"Well, what happened next?" I asked, by now certain that they hadn't stopped there.

"By this time, we'd gone from a 3.0 Sigma to a 4.7 to a 5.0. We didn't have that many problems left—at least not obvious ones—so we decided to make a solution for a problem we really didn't have. One of my Green Belts—who is now a Black Belt—gave me an idea: Why not just keep making pizzas during lunch and dinner rush hours, whether we had the orders or not?"

"Now *that* sounds ridiculous," I said.

"That's what I thought!" Larry said. "But not after she explained it. Her thinking went like this: Instead of *waiting* for orders to come in when we're busiest, just keep making the most popular pizzas—which we could determine statistically with our computers—until someone came up to order them. Keep the wheels turning that way and get the customers and pizzas out of the way when a big party with tricky orders shows up. You've got the room to accommodate them."

"That's fine," I said. "But what if no one buys the pizzas you're making? You just eat 'em, as it were?"

"Good question," Larry said. "But she had all the right answers. First of all, even if we did have to eat them, we had gotten the cost of making them down so low that we'd still be better off, because we were moving so much faster during most rush hours. But she had a great backup idea, too. The ones we didn't sell as whole pizzas, she said, we could sell by the slice at our walk-up windows—with a much higher markup, by the way, than a whole pizza and less cost, because we didn't have to deliver it. Of course, we had to invent the walk-up window, too!"

"Incredible," I whispered. "How long did this take?"

"All of it?" he asked. "The whole thing, every project I mentioned, was completed in about two-and-a-half years."

"Geez! What do you do for an encore?"

"Well, the walk-up business got to be so brisk, we had to keep buying more conveyor-belt ovens. And then we decided our biggest problem was our stores were too small to handle the demand. So we expanded the walk-up window into a sit-down area, and now we're turning those areas into restaurants—that's what we're sitting in right now!"

I almost choked on my pizza.

"That's how American Pizza started its restaurants?!"

"Afraid so, buddy!" he said. "One thing led to another."

"Guess so," I said. "What do you have now, about a thousand stores?"

"A little over," he replied. "And we're going to double in the next three years. We've added sit-down restaurants to about 30 stores, and almost all of the new ones will be restaurants, too."

"What about Six Sigma?" I asked. "Get there yet?"

"No, not yet," Larry reported. "Year by year we rose from 3.0 to 3.4 to 3.8 to 4.7 to 5.0, but we ran into diminishing returns, just like anything else."

"So that's as far as you can go?"

"Actually, no!" he said. "You *can* get to Six Sigma, but you have to take an even more advanced approach."

Susan, the waitress, didn't bring over the bill until Larry motioned for it, as is the custom in Europe. The message is: No rush, take your time. You're important here.

But instead of a bill, Susan presented us with a comment card with a dollar paper-clipped to it. "I want to thank you in advance for filling out this card," she said to me. "And when you're done, please accept this crisp new one dollar bill as our thank you!"

After she left, I asked, "Man, does this really work?" My cynicism hadn't disappeared altogether.

"94 percent of the time!" Larry said. "Turns out, when you treat customers right, they have consciences. And don't be fooled. We raised our prices about 75 cents on a $15 meal, so this really only costs us a quarter. Twenty-five cents to pick our customers' brains, we decided, was easily worth it."

"Hmmm," I uttered, as he handed me the pencil to fill out the card. "But wait a second, where's the bill?"

"I've already charged it to my account, my friend," he said. "Customers told us they liked to have an in-store account, like Bloomingdale's. So you've just enjoyed the proverbial free lunch!"

"Thank you," I said, sincerely. My mood had improved significantly for a man who'd been let go earlier that day. In fact, I had barely even thought of that whole mess since Larry started explaining Six Sigma to me. Not that I really wanted to, either. I shook the thought. "But where do you fit into the whole Six Sigma thing now?" I asked. "Still doing projects?"

"Not directly," he said. "After a couple years as a Black Belt, directing the projects we talked about, Cathy decided to promote me to Master Black Belt. After the honchos at American Food's headquarters saw what we were doing, they wanted to expand the program. Trust me, it wasn't hard recruiting Black Belts the next time around. No one worried that being picked was the kiss of death!"

"No, I suppose not," I said. I found myself feeling *envious*. I would like to have been asked to become a Black Belt!

"Sounds like you wouldn't mind being tapped for Black Belt school yourself," Larry said.

"Actually," I said, "and you're not going to believe this—I was just thinking that. I was pretty skeptical when you started talking about all this."

"I noticed," he added, with understated humor. "But look at you now."

"I know," I said. I was surprised to feel like an eager recruit, chomping at the bit to put on the varsity uniform.

"Seems like you understand the whole Six Sigma approach pretty well by now," Larry added.

"I guess I do," I said, "despite my efforts to the contrary! I think I might actually believe in it."

"Nooo!" Larry said, with mock incredulity. "Shame on you for believing in a new quality initiative!"

"What can I say?" I admitted, palms up. "You made a persuasive case."

"I'm curious if you could sum it up for me," he said. "Not to test you, but to see if I got it across accurately."

> **"A**s I understand it, the main thrust of Six Sigma is to reduce errors and waste in every kind of business endeavor to please customers and fatten the bottom line."

"Okay," I said. "Since *you're* the one being tested! As I understand it, the main thrust of Six Sigma is to reduce errors and waste in every kind of business endeavor to please customers and fatten the bottom line."

"So far, so good," he said, mimicking my response from earlier in the day.

"You do that not simply by cranking up quality control, but by taking a step back, *defining* where the *underlying* problems are—within the business, process, or operation—and eliminating them."

"Good," he said.

I held a finger up to indicate I wasn't done. "The key to doing all *that,* of course, is *measuring* where you are and where you want to go, *analyzing* the data, *improving* the situation, and *controlling* the activity after you fix it to make sure you don't slip."

"Excellent!" Larry said. "Now, how do you accomplish all that?"

I didn't miss a beat. "You give everyone on board very specific jobs and rewards—recognition, promotion, bonuses—for doing them well. The Black Belt, especially, needs to be given all the resources necessary to focus solely on making the Six Sigma project a success. And you know, it occurs to me, the *power* of Six Sigma is that everyone throughout the corporation is speaking the same language—the language of Six Sigma."

"Bravo!" he said, only half tongue-in-cheek, while clapping. "Well done, my friend. You sound like a half Six Sigma graduate! But you've got to do a real-life project with documented cost savings to become a *full* graduate."

Larry leaned forward on his elbows and spoke softly, almost conspiratorially. "You know, the top brass at American Foods were so impressed by what Cathy had done in the pizza division that they promoted her to the central office last year, where she started shaking things up there.

"The next stop, she says, is to improve from Five to Six Sigma—and the only way to get there is through Design For Six Sigma, or DFSS."

"Now," I asked, "how does *that* work?"

Looking at his watch, Larry replied, "That, my friend, is another story, for another day. But do me a favor," he added, looking me in the eyes. "Keep in touch. You never know what's going to happen next."

ACKNOWLEDGMENTS

Over the years, I've been influenced by and learned from many individuals. I would like to extend enormous gratitude to the man who taught all of us the power of quality—Dr. W. Edwards Deming. He would have celebrated his 100th birthday the year this book was written. I am very fortunate to work very closely with Dr. Genichi Taguchi—his teaching inspires me every day. Dr. Armand V. Feigenbaum, Philip B. Crosby, and J. D. Power III have also been a great inspiration to me—their continuous support of my work is extremely valuable. I honor and respect all of them.

For the development and production of this book I feel a deep sense of gratitude to:

- My friend, John Bacon, for his enormous support and hard work from day one, and for helping me refine the manuscript with integrity and a sense of quality.

- My Dearborn Trade editor, Jean Iversen Cook, for her professional competence and project leadership, and for her continuous challenge. Jean is a true Black Belt editor.

- My very special friend in the publishing business, Cynthia Zigmund, publisher at Dearborn Trade, for her belief in every one of my writing ventures from the first day I met her, and for her continuous encouragement.

- Everyone at Dearborn Trade for their hard work: Sandy Thomas, Leslie Banks, Robin Nominelli, Mindi Rowland, Paul Mallon, and Jack Kiburz.

- My friend, Robert MacLeod, for his constant support of my work, who put aside his own needs in order to help me.

- My friend, Ken Zimmer, for his suggestions on the manuscript and his continuous encouragement.

- My dear friends and colleagues in the business, especially everyone at ASI—American Supplier Institute—for their assistance and help and for all of their suggestions on the manuscript: Shin

Taguchi, Alan Wu, Jim Wilkins, Jodi Caldwell, Melanie Peters, Tim Stacey, and Esmeralda Facundo.

- All my friends at Delphi Automotive Systems, Ford Motor Company, and General Motors, for their valuable advice on the manuscript.

- My friend, John King, for his detailed review on the first draft.

- All my friends in the Six Sigma business, including AIT Group, BMG, and George Group for their continuous support.

- Four of my colleagues, Ki Chang, Jef Spencer, John Terninko, and Barry Bebb, for their dedication on Six Sigma and DFSS activities.

I am also eternally grateful to my parents, Sushil and Krishna Chowdhury, for their constant demonstrations of love, and to my in-laws, Ashim and Krishna Guha. Most of all, my heartfelt thanks to my wonderful wife, Malini, for her blind support on each of my projects.

ABOUT THE AUTHOR

Subir Chowdhury is executive vice president at the American Supplier Institute, an international consulting and training firm for Six Sigma and quality. Prior to ASI, he served as a quality management consultant at General Motors Corporation. Hailed by the *New York Times* as a "Leading Quality Expert," Chowdhury was also recognized by *Quality Progress* of the American Society for Quality as one of the "Voices of Quality in the 21st Century."

He has received numerous international awards for his leadership in quality management and major contributions to the automotive industry. Chowdhury was honored by the Automotive Hall of Fame, and the Society of Automotive Engineers awarded him its most prestigious recognition, the Henry Ford II Distinguished Award for Excellence in automotive engineering. He also received the honorable U.S. Congressional Recognition.

Chowdhury is the author, coauthor, or editor of *Robust Engineering, QS-9000 Pioneers, Management 21C,* and *The Mahalanobis-Taguchi System.* In 1999–2000, he served as chairman of the American Society for Quality's Automotive Division.

He lives with his wife, Malini, in Novi, Michigan.

Six Sigma . . . Simplified

Share *The Power of Six Sigma* with the rest of your company!

For quantity discounts of *The Power of Six Sigma,* please contact Mindi Rowland in Special Sales, 800-621-9621, ext. 4410, rowland@dearborn.com. Your company can also order this book with a customized cover featuring your name, logo, and message.

Dearborn™
Trade Publishing
A **Kaplan Professional** Company